Living the Quaker Way

Ben Pink Dandelion

For all of us

First published May 2012

Quaker Books, Friends House, 173 Euston Road, London NW1 2BJ

Enquiries should be addressed to the Publications Manager, Quaker Books, Friends House, 173 Euston Road, London NW1 2BJ.

www.quaker.org.uk

ISBN 978 1 907123 27 6

Introduction

This pocket-sized book is a companion volume to *Celebrating the Quaker Way*, which first appeared in 2009. The aim of that volume, as its title suggests, was to celebrate the wonderful riches of our Quaker tradition. When in drafts I strayed from celebration to explanation, my editors kindly scored through the offending text, allowing the end product to remain purely a celebratory text for all of us who enjoy the Quaker way.

This book contains explanation. It explores why we do the things we do in the way that we do them. It is still celebratory but also looks at why and how we live our Quaker faith. It is a book about us and for us, based on the Quaker way in Britain. I have tried to keep history to a minimum as we have our own reasons for our present-day faith and practice. It talks of 'us' and 'we' and is for 'insiders'. It is a devotional book, for us.

As I wrote in the earlier book, "I talk of God in the way Friends have traditionally talked of the Divine, although some today may prefer other terms, and I hope that those readers can 'translate' or hear where the words come from, as they might approach ministry in meeting for worship. I write as a Quaker who came to meeting as an atheist/agnostic, drawn in by the peace testimony, an ex-anarchist, happy to find another place without leaders and without votes. Two years in, I had an experience aboard a Greyhound bus in America that gave me a sense of being lifted up, held, and since then perpetually accompanied by what I call God, but which I know is ultimately a mystery that is not for me to know too closely. Thus, Quakerism moved for me from being a primarily political affiliation to a place where I could connect and reconnnect with that grace-filled sense of being watched over, guarded and guided. It has fitted me not only intellectually but practically in my life of faith. It gives me exactly the form of worship and the opportunity for expression and service that matches my own experience of direct inward encounter".

We all have a ministry, or a series of ministries, each for its season, where we use the spiritual gifts given us by God. This book is written as part of my ongoing ministry. It draws on my experience of Quakerism, and extracts from Friends talking on these topics recorded for the book (these Friends' words are in quotation marks). I hope I have been faithful to what has been given me, a twig on the ocean.

The book is divided into three sections. The first is about the inward nature of Quaker spirituality. The second is about the way this informs how we worship and the way we conduct our business through worship. The third part is on how the boundlessness of God's invitation to all of us dramatically affects our view of our neighbours, and of how we are to live in and with 'the world' (the non-Quaker society we are a part of, but so often informed by a different set of values).

Questions on each section for personal reflection and to encourage discussion in our meetings complete the book.

I thank Woodbrooke Quaker Study Centre in Birmingham and my family for giving me the space and encouragement to write this, participants in the November 2011 Pendle Hill course 'And then I heard a voice' for their support and input, and those who read earlier drafts and gave me so much help.

1 Inward spirituality

We are Quakers. We worship in a way different from those around us and often our lives feel particular too. For some of us our experience of worship leads to our lifestyle, for others our lifestyle is affirmed by what we find in the silence. For others still, both combine.

Whether our Quaker life is fired from a sense of presence or by a sense of how to live in the world, the foundational Quaker insight is that this 'knowing' is experienced inwardly. It is a knowing of the heart, not the head. We need no outward guides, people or text to lead us into this place of encounter and understanding. Instead we rely particularly on outward absence to release us to a sense of inward presence. We find stillness and silence the best preparation for and the best means to a deeper experience of the spiritual life. Set free and cast away from the world and its concerns, we come to navigate layers of silence to reach towards the mystery and unknowability of God. We sink down within ourselves to find that which we cannot ever fully fathom. We engage in expectant waiting and listening.

Quaker founder George Fox had his first sense of encounter in 1647 when "my hopes in all men were gone" and "I had nothing outwardly to help me". Then he heard a voice, which told him that there was "one, even Christ Jesus" that could speak to his condition, and his "heart did leap for joy". Fox learnt first-hand, as generations of us have since, that having nothing outwardly to help us opens the way to the draught of God's love. God comes to us in the silence and the stillness, and in that place of inward quiet we come to experience God and hear what God is calling us to. The outward is not just unnecessary but also unhelpful. "I've found that [education and learning] is a deceptive path . . . It doesn't really lead to any depth. The Quaker way . . . helps you sink deeper into a way of knowing that moves you out of a rational realm into a deeper way of knowing. It's threatening; I like my false sense of security [but] . . . I try to just let go and surrender . . . I sense that it's right . . . and the Quaker path gives you space to do that."

Many of us are alive with a sense of God's love even amidst busy and noisy lives. We find a holy pace and a small, still centre is present even when all is outwardly elsewhere. God's accompaniment can be wonderfully persistent throughout all kinds of hubbub and thicken even through slumber. "Sometimes I'm called into worship in the middle of the night. I bundle up, go downstairs, and settle into worship. Recently, after a workshop about God's presence, I returned home and had this sense I needed to sit in worship. I got a really clear sense that to change my outward life I had to accept the grace within."

Silence comes easily and naturally to us and we have persisted with it as the basis for worship for over 350 years because it works. The postcard reads "I am a Quaker – in case of emergency, please be quiet". Faced with crisis, we fall to silence. We turn to God to ask for help. Silence is how we approach the Divine collectively, how in those intentional and together-hoped-for moments of sacramental encounter we choose to pray and listen and rest awhile in the tenderness of God's love. "For years, I thought an encounter with the Divine would be huge, a big experience, and that everything would be suddenly clear, but what I've discovered is that simply being faithful day after day boosts the still small voice – there are no cymbals, no thunder."

We know, in both head and heart, that we do not need a minister to preach to us. We have no need to all sing together, or take part in any outward ritual. Those things may help us prepare for the communion we find in the silence, as they do for Quakers in other parts of the world, but are only ever the means to prepare for encounter, not the encounter itself. "We are called to be naked in our worship, both free from our earthly concerns and without the ritual and forms that some in other Churches rely upon." There is no need to mark outwardly what is felt so keenly within. There is no need for outward remembrance of something not forgotten. When we know 'of God', we know of the Divine directly and unforgettably. We know inwardly at both a personal and collective level. "I will never be alone again."

☙

Importantly, this approach to God is available to everyone. God's invitation to intimacy is, wonderfully, given to us all.

The spiritual opportunity is universal. Thus, George Fox had no claim to spiritual authority above any other Quaker. He had no special or particular relationship with God but in his moment of brokenness, of openness, discovered God's wonderful, ongoing and fulsome invitation to the whole of humanity. This is an invitation that in its direct and inward nature steers us away from unhelpful adulation of others or pride within. Simply, we are called to be faithful vessels of God's loving ministry, one to another.

We all are blessed with gifts to help further God's loving purposes, we all have a ministry. Our sense of vocation may be life-long or be made up of a series of new calls. "I know I'm a teacher, that's my ministry. But that's not the only gift or ministry I have . . . I'm waiting for an answer as to what is next . . . in the form of an opening." We can be called like Mary without any sense of choice, or like Moses where there appeared to be choice, or be offered a genuine choice by God, or discover, delightfully, that we are already living our call: "I used to wonder what I was going to be when I grew up. I spent three years on a quest to find out . . . it finally occurred to me that the life I'm in right now is my ministry. Surrendering is not an intellectual experience. When I finally was able to let go, I realised the life I'm living was it . . . it is unbelievably exciting to surrender and let life take me where it will." We are not to be shy of the power and authority of the gifts we are given but joyfully surrender to the life we are called to lead, and use those gifts humbly and obediently.

We are all invited into the corporate encounter with God. In traditional Christian terms, we are all saved, all loved. Equally, we are all responsible, all part of the corporate priesthood realising God's kingdom in all we do and say. "It's taken me a long time to understand how sitting in prayer or contemplation *among* other people is different from sitting in prayer or contemplation *with* other people." The Quaker way is not to be lived apart. We enact our faith, called to a life of justice, compassion, joy and prayerful attention amongst our community and amidst the challenges of the everyday. God calls us, all of us, directly. Our role is to respond.

2   Worship

We call the grace we are given to respond to God "that of God in everyone". It is not about God being within all, but about the ability to experience God within and in turn to take up our part in the priesthood. "In meeting, if I can silence my ego, my stuff, I can actually hear – and in the hearing, connect to others. When I can be present, I feel God's presence."

Living out our faith as a 'priesthood of all believers' gives us options when it comes to worship. We could ask the person with a gift of nurturing worship to take that role on for us (akin to Quaker pastors in the majority of the Quaker world, or elders), or we could rotate the leadership of worship week by week. However, the reliability of silence and stillness, the direct inward nature of divine leadership we regularly experience, and the fact that we are all ministers, has led us for over 350 years to employ and enjoy 'open' or 'unprogrammed' worship and a 'free ministry'. In other words, we choose worship based in silence without rite or rote, with words (vocal ministry) only shared when *any* one of us feels led to offer them.

The first consequence of this is that there is no 'front' to a Quaker meeting as there is no one or no-thing to face. Typically we worship in a circle or a square denoting how we come before the Holy Other as equals, each with our shortcomings and our skills, frustrated hopes and wildest dreams, our longing for God. Second, there is no need for anything to be said or done outwardly. We simply surrender ourselves to experience, the play of God's Light on the depths of our being. Silence and stillness nurture the sense of presence, and anything that is spoken is to add to the riches we find in the silence. Third, in that place of encounter and transformation, we are called to discern whether what we feel led to share is really ministry. Is this a message from God or a response to somebody else's ministry? Is it repetition? Is it a bright idea? Is it only about me? If it is a message from God, is it to be shared outwardly? With this group? At this time? Through me? If yes, we need to faithfully relay what we have been given. Sometimes, whilst we are still discerning, someone else is on their feet expressing the very sentiments we had been given, or the moment clearly passes and we were rightly silent.

ᑳ

So, worship begins in quiet, the silence tending the stilling and the stilling tending the silence. Friends have different ways into the silence, of 'centring down'. Some of us start by praying for everyone else there, others of us follow a personal meditation to help move us across from all our thoughts and concerns, and still others of us find it possible to simply sink into the silence, to 'keep low' and withdraw from our selves before God. Practice helps. Silence is not easy but also cannot be feigned: in the midst of divine encounter, we know when we are there. When the whole group reaches that place, the meeting is called 'gathered' or 'covered'. As we become practised at worship, so we get more and more from these intentional moments of corporate response to God's loving invitation. "The experience of other silences is not the same . . . Quaker silence is different. It brings peace."

When we are given ministry to share, we typically stand to offer it so as to be better heard and to help us remember what we are about; the free ministry is potentially risky and Quaker writers have talked about "the dangers of silent worship": we could easily fill worship with talk or good ideas and turn our back on the Divine or crowd God out. To nurture our expectant waiting, we leave spaces between ministry to reflect on what has been shared, avoid speaking right at the beginning or right at the end, and only minister once in a meeting. God may give us much to say but we are encouraged to distil it into as few words as possible or let it mature for a future meeting. In large meetings, we are encouraged to remain silent if we are unsure if what we have to say is really ministry. In smaller meetings, perhaps hungry for vocal ministry to help feed the discipline of our inward communion, we might say "If in doubt, do!" My own small meeting often starts with a reading to help us towards the attention we need to give to quieting ourselves before God, and to encourage vocal ministry.

We are given ministry by grace to share freely. It may be helpful to some but not all and it is not for us to judge it. As ministry is not discussion or response, so it does not lead to discussion or response. Most people are clear when they have shared ministry and some find themselves on their feet before they are aware of very much at all. "I feel a leading – whether to speak in meeting or something larger – first as a funny internal wiggle that eventually grows into a full body awareness. Sometimes when I become totally clear and follow a leading I may cry a bit because it's so powerful."

We appoint elders from amongst us to help nurture our worship, to encourage ministry from the tentative, and to remind us if we minister when things were better left unsaid. On rare occasions, elders interrupt a long ministry to help restore the silence for the rest of the group. It is a difficult step to take as ministry is, in theory, divinely inspired and the elders need to practise their own discernment whether or not to act.

Elders 'close' or end worship by shaking hands. In the past half-century, everyone has taken to following this lead. We greet each other, welcome each other back into the world, and give thanks for the worship we have shared and the community we feel part of. Worship is typically an hour but may extend if there is much ministry or ministry right at the end. Time is only outward and ending worship at a particular time is far less important than being open to the winds of the Spirit.

The same discipline applies to our meetings for worship for marriage or to give thanks for the life of a departed Friend. We witness to what God is giving to us inwardly in the silence and outwardly through vocal ministry. The outward is a reflection of the inward spiritual reality. Our outward expression reflects what God is realising, making real, in, through, and amongst us, whether it be a call to action, gratitude for a faithful life, or the marriage by God of two of our number. The dynamic heart of all of our meetings is inward encounter and outward expression, the recognition, celebration and outworking of all that is given by God.

CB

Discernment is central to the Quaker way. Without the mediation of text or minister, we need to work out for ourselves what is and what is not of God. Discernment is the key discipline to accompany the claim that God's guidance is available to us all individually, the responsibility that accompanies the gift of grace. Like silence, it is something we work on and develop our skills in. We need to 'test' what is given us, in and through our own spiritual experience but also in and through the spiritual experience of others in our community. This is not always possible and we may only realise the faithfulness of an action retrospectively – the rush of energy, the flow of positive consequences like a row of falling dominoes, or the fruits of the Spirit that follow a rightly led decision or the opposite for one that was not. We discern if and when to minister in meeting, elders discern when to act in meeting, and we may hold a 'clearness meeting' to discern with others whether we are truly led and 'clear' to marry, or whether or not to take a new job. We are not necessarily seeking answers but we are trying to know what it is to be faithful, what it means to be true to the Spirit.

"About five years ago I went to a monastery and ran into a Benedictine monk who'd been there for sixty years. I asked him how he discerned, how he sought the will of God. He said, 'I don't . . . ask for guidance. I don't pray. It's just there.' . . . He was just living it out . . . Being in the silence has been challenging for me, but there's an inner observer there that . . . shines a light on my more selfish tendencies."

As a people continually open to and led by the Spirit, we are continually discerning. Without discernment, our discipleship fails, our worship fails and we are left with only a secular shadow. We need to be open to God and prepared to wrestle with the temptations of our own imaginations.

ᙙ

When we engage with our meetings for business or 'church affairs', we are involved in a discernment process based in worship. In traditional Quaker terms, we are seeking the will of God. In the past decades this phrase has been variously interpreted, as Quaker theology has become more diverse. For some Friends, 'God' is an unhelpful term or they believe in a God that does not have a will. For others, 'will' means different things, ranging from where God has an answer to every question, to broad brush preferences whereby we are left to sort out the detail. For others, God learns as we do and God's will is co-created. Whatever our theology of God's will, we know we best find the way forward by entering into worship.

We appoint a 'clerk' to help us maintain our discipline in meetings for worship for business, although elders also nurture the worship and support 'the table'. The clerk does not lead but 'serves', helping us remember our process and what we are about. We worship, pray, and listen for divine nudgings and promptings and when led, we rise to offer ministry to help the meeting forward. In larger gatherings, more than one Friend may stand at the same time and the clerk discerns who to 'call'. As with all vocal ministry, our spoken contributions are usually short and concise. Silence ensues before another ministry is prompted, another of us called. Contributions are addressed to the clerk and as in all worship, this is not a time for conversation or discussion. We are involved in a God-guided process, not a task. We are not engaged in finding a solution to a problem but seeking to know what God is calling us to at this time. The clerk's role is to discern the 'sense of the meeting' based on the ministry and to record this in a 'minute'. The clerk prepares and reads a draft of the minute when they feel the time is right and the discernment continues on the minute, no longer the matter. "I love to clerk business meetings – I find Jesus Christ sitting next to me. It gives me phenomenal courage to get out of the way. It is so not like me to have Jesus Christ in my life. That is when I am most aware of the Divine, when I am most trusting, when I am at my best."

The clerk drafts the minute and asks "Is the minute acceptable?" and if it is 'good enough', we reply "Hope so". Personally, we hope it is, and collectively, we hope we have discerned correctly. None of us claim to know God's will so well as to call out "Yes!" The minute is only accepted if everyone or virtually everyone is in agreement or agrees to agree. This may mean that if a few of us cannot agree on a minute, the decision does not go ahead.

As God's will is seen to be singular, so finding the sense of the meeting on an item is seen to represent a rightly discerned decision. We do not vote on business items and not being in unity may tell us the discernment is not complete. Sometimes a small minority hold out for a decision that eventually the large body comes to see is 'in right ordering' (in God's ordering). As a religious society, the decision may not be the most rational, logical or even outwardly sensible, but it is what we hope and believe God wants us to do. I remember a Friend rising and saying: "If we were the Society of Friends I would oppose this proposal as risky and irrational but we are the Religious Society of Friends and I am feeling strongly led that we should accept this proposal." Yearly Meeting in session is regularly inspiring. Gatherings of over one thousand Friends finding the sense of the meeting on a difficult issue is always affirming of our ability to enact our discipleship and discern faithfully. "Most of my experiences of God at work have been in big meetings for worship for business. You feel it, you know. While we've done our homework and preparation on a subject, the timing is unexpected. This happened with the issue of gay and lesbian unions in our meeting. Suddenly Friends were moving into unity. There's an amazing joy, the feeling of the

Spirit filling the room and spreading out to all those in our community beyond those present in the room. Surprise and joy are the hallmarks for me of God's guidance. It feels right."

We are not to know where we may be led and we may come to see that our hopes were for things way beyond our imagination. "There are God-incidents (not coincidences) in life. Something is at work through life. The common pattern is being surprised . . . and grateful." What is important is being faithful to the next step and knowing we take it not in our power but in God's.

⚃

Our structure, and the way of doing business through the testing of leadings, is largely unchanged from the early Quaker vision of 'Gospel Order'. In other words, our system of 'church government' reflects how we feel God wants the Quaker Church to be organised. It is a decentralised pattern with most decisions taken locally. Each meeting is based on a flat structure; we are levelled down before the leadership of God or the Spirit.

As a group focused on the inward encounter, all of the outward forms of worship are to some extent pragmatic. Some habits, like the recent practice of having flowers on the table in the middle, have no theological logic, they simply appeal. Some meetings experiment with all-age worship where the children and young people stay and contribute to the meeting rather than attending 'children's class'. Others experiment with untimed worship or meetings lasting three hours as they used to. Some have abandoned all local committees when faced with difficulty filling them and reworked their volunteering around their most pressing needs. Some, keen to reduce their carbon footprint, now meet on Saturdays instead of Sundays so Friends have access to better public transport. Quakerism is our attempt at collective congruity with the workings of the Spirit and it can change as it needs to. The future of how we practise our faith lies in all of our hands and hearts, in our collective discernment. There is no 'they' in Quakerism, only 'us', and we are all learning all the time, open to new Light, continuing to seek along the spiritual path we call the Quaker way. Wonderfully, we regularly find the totally unexpected and the totally amazing, such are its abundant riches.

3 Life

Our spiritual experience draws us closer to God. When we
experience intimacy with the Divine, we are given a sense of
God that is beyond words and beyond full understanding.
Whilst earlier generations of Quakers were very sure about
what they believed, we are clear that we cannot be wholly
or finally sure about doctrine. We each make sense of our
spiritual experience but we do not imagine that the way we
understand the holy is necessarily right for anyone else. We
are sure for ourselves or sure partially or sure provisionally,
for now, but not sure completely or for everyone or for all time.
Paradoxically, we feel pretty certain about this at-least partial
uncertainty. In this way, our beliefs are 'towards' or 'perhaps'
kind of ones and we are cautious about anyone who claims
they have the final word of God or can totally understand
God and God's ways. "It is possible to be open and ardent at
the same time. Too often, those who are ardent are closed
off. To be open as a Quaker one has to listen. Your meeting
holds your feet to the fire. It's the only place I've found this
connection."

Our open worship accommodates our theological diversity.
We agree how to worship and how to do business, in other
words how to make space to experience God. We are also clear
that speaking of religious belief always falls short because
the words we have never match the depth of that experience.
Quakers have never adopted a creed. Quaker faith is revealed

by our lives, not language. We minister in different theological dialects and become adept at translating the meaning of the ministry into our own spiritual language, or of feeling beyond and behind it. "When I started going to meeting, I kept wanting to go back. Becoming part of the community was like a promise to myself. It was a spiritual promise to search and be part of a community. Being surrounded by those people has been a huge blessing that has changed my life . . . has brought me to a real faith. Just reading books about spirituality would not have brought me to the same place. It wouldn't have happened." The Quaker way is not about profession but possession. We let our lives preach.

⚃

The idea of "that of God in everyone" and the spiritual equality that accompanies this idea of the universal elect means that everyone is equally important. Each of us is a unique and precious child of God. Thus, we have always opposed killing and war and anything which diminishes another. Our witness, our testimony, is the way we live because spiritually we can do no other. "When I left the Protestant Church, I was looking for simplicity, peace and equality. I needed those." Our tradition and practice encourages and affirms us to lead a spiritual life embedded in how God is calling us to live. "The work that I do is with people. When we connect, we grow God in the world." We become testimony.

We are less wary of 'the world' than the earlier Friends. They wore Quaker grey as a plain form of dress, refused to use the pagan names for days and months or use titles or the deferential 'you', preferring 'thee' and 'thou'. In their levelling of society, they eschewed worldly manners such as bowing or the doffing of a hat. They outlawed for themselves music and theatre and novels. They refused to pay tithes to the "hireling ministry" or swear in court because of the injunction in the book of Matthew's gospel not to swear and because they said they told the truth all of the time. We still affirm in court but have become freer about how we dress and also about music and the arts, feeling we can maintain our integrity inwardly and enjoy these outward forms. We are less worried about emotions and 'self' getting in the way of our relationship to God than our forebears. We have translated the ideal of plainness into simplicity and being 'against war' into being 'for peace'. We are more relaxed about 'marrying out' (marrying a non-Quaker), which led to thousands leaving Quakerism. Indeed, many of us are now married to or in partnership with non-Quakers and in the last one hundred years a dynastic and familial Quakerism has been replaced by 85 per cent of us becoming Friends as adults. We are very clear we want to be engaged with the world and that our faith needs to be relevant to the age.

Early Quakers did not have a membership system; it was obvious by dress and speech who was and who was not a Quaker. In the 1730s, British Quakers made up lists to work out which meeting would give poor relief to which Quaker families and, by default, 'membership lists' were created. Children were automatically listed as members until 1959. Today, people apply for membership as it helps them be clear to themselves and the world that they are Quakers. It denotes no greater spiritual development or maturity but is a public statement of saying we understand the Quaker way and are committed to it. It is about being part of the priesthood and sharing the service that our collective work and worship requires. "It's not being a member that's important, it is what being a member stands for." At the same time, everyone is equal before God and, members or not, we are a single community of worshippers bound together by the riches of all we experience and the desire to discern how we are to live our faith. "I've found [in Quaker meeting] . . . a sense of being held, and it seems authentic."

However, alongside a more relaxed approach to how and who we are, we are also clear that there is much about modern consumer culture that we cannot support or participate in. We work for a more just and peaceful world, one with less discrimination and greater equality, a more sustainable approach to the economy and to the planet, and a greater degree of integrity amongst those entrusted with power and responsibility. We feel these certainties deeply, beyond conscious choice. These values are who we are. They affect what we buy and where we shop, how or if we travel, how we are in the workplace. We try not to be dissuaded from doing the right thing just because it is unpopular. We are active in all kinds of organisations to try to achieve these ends, not in our own power, but based on the holy imperatives given us in worship. We care passionately.

Knowing how to act and when calls for discernment. Some moral dilemmas are not easy. Do we hide refugees facing death even if it means lying to the authorities? How far can we maintain our testimony against violence and killing if our families are threatened? We cannot say until faced with the situation and we have taken individual paths as we have felt led. Thus, we do not agree on everything. We have different views on alcohol or the lottery. Some have difficulty with pacifism, and in the two World Wars many individuals joined up whilst others went to prison as conscientious objectors. Each of us is called to try to discern the right course and we can ask little more of each other than the sincere attempt to get it as right as we can, to keep discerning. We need each other to help test our different leadings and to be here for each other when we get things wrong, as we do and will: we are not Quakers together because we are 'good' but because we are not. "Quakers need to be in community for fellowship, decision-making and support."

We share a strongly felt optimism about humanity and human potential and with it an overwhelming compassion for each other and the rest of humanity, our neighbours in the widest sense. "I grew up in a Quaker family. There was a feeling that there was a lot to be thankful for. I learned to be kind to the animals. It wasn't difficult to attend meeting. It was a way of life around the farm." We are called to help create a loving society.

ଓ

Our spiritual experience leads us to new levels or inward sites of spiritual relationship which are continuous. George Fox talked about being taken through "the flaming sword" back into the Garden of Eden and other early Friends talked of being made anew. In a less dramatic way, I have felt God's accompaniment in my life daily since that day I was unexpectedly lifted out of my seat on the Greyhound bus, held, and encouraged towards a new life by what has been a very patient teacher! We keep trying to live the faithful life and we keep learning the faithful life.

My experience of an accompanied life is not true for everyone but we are clear that a life of trying to live God's loving purposes is not limited to the Sunday morning or midweek meeting. We are called to witness to those purposes all of the time, to help the kingdom unfold in the here and now. Early Quakers never developed a theology of the afterlife because they never imagined they needed one: they had such a strong sense of the world being turned upside down in the 1650s that the New Jerusalem would be realised in their lifetime. The world did not change as much as they imagined and 'Gospel Order' and the building of meeting houses from the 1670s was one consequence of realising it was a longer journey.

The witness of our everyday lives continues and is continuous, but we feel the urgency to transform the world as keenly as our forebears.

Quaker silence always has consequences. The inward leads to the outward. As we listen to what God is calling us to, there will always be more to know and more to realise, make real. Faithful living is always an ongoing process, a joyful and necessarily continuous witness to the expression of God's love for all of humanity. "God is not 'encounters' for me, it's something right there over my shoulder and accessible at any time."

We may travel to the historic Quaker sites to get a better sense of the first years of Quakerism but no place is any more sacred than any other: we do not have a theology of pilgrimage. Rather, everywhere is a 'thin place' where we can connect with the majesty of mystical experience. Similarly, all times are equally special and we meet when it is convenient to do so. Early Quakers were criticised for opening their shops on Christmas Day. Today, some of us celebrate Christmas but no day is more sacred than any other. Every day is Christmas and Easter, such is the power, reach and continuity of our intimacy with God. "I feel that God or the Spirit is my constant companion – that I am accompanied, surrounded." We live in God's time.

༄

Early Quakers had a mission to the world. They felt they were the true Church and everyone could be and needed to be saved. The kingdom of heaven was to be realised on earth. British Quakers today talk little of salvation but we maintain a sense of outreach to everyone, a present-day version of our good news. "I have no reservations about the good news of Quakerism. There are lots of people looking for what we have to offer. The Quaker way lets people experience God directly, letting everyone take responsibility for their spiritual growth." We have a unique approach to worship and to the nature of religious belief, a particular understanding of connection with God and of being a people of God. We have a key focus on discerning what God is calling us to do and proven methods for realising that collective seeking, and a strong set of spiritual values aimed at making the world a better place for all of creation.

We live the Quaker way. Every day. We are the Quaker way.

Reflection and discussion

The following questions are designed to help you reflect on your own experience of what you value, celebrate and understand for yourself about the Quaker way.

They can be used either for individual reflection, or by small groups.

If you are meeting as a group, agree some ground rules at the beginning. Important ones might be to allow everyone a chance to speak, to speak only from your own experience, and that no one has to speak if they don't want to.

Make sure that the book and the questions are accessible to anyone not able to read print, either by obtaining an audio version or reading relevant sections aloud in the group.

If the group is large, you may wish to spend some time in twos, threes or fours before returning to the large group.

Choose between worship sharing or group discussion. Groups may prefer one or the other. Some dislike the discipline of worship sharing when they are bursting with ideas; some find it difficult to contribute in a discussion if they are not given a specific space to do so. Be sensitive to everyone's needs.

Questions for reflection and discussion

1. Inward spirituality

   a) Think of moments when the Spirit has been at work in your life or when you have felt closest to the Divine. What was it like? Is there any pattern?

   b) What are your gifts? What is your ministry?

   c) How do you nurture your spirituality?

   d) What does the Quaker way give you?

2. Worship

   a) What is your experience of worship? What words do you use to describe it?

   b) How do you make decisions in your life? Does anyone from meeting help you?

   c) What are business meetings like in your meeting? Is there anything you would like to change?

   d) What helps you discern?

3. Life

   a) Do you do anything differently as a consequence of attending Quaker meeting?

   b) Does coming to Quaker meeting help you in your life? If so, how? Do you feel supported by your meeting in the choices you make?

   c) What is your vision for Quakerism? How are we going to get there?

   d) What is the good news about Quakerism for you? What do you want to tell others about?

Milton Keynes UK
Ingram Content Group UK Ltd
UKHW021352260524
443099UK00015B/563

9 781907 123276